DEBT PAYOFF
TRACKER LOG

THIS BOOK BELONGS TO

NAME : _____

CONTACT : _____

ADDRESS : _____

Debt Payoff

CREDITOR:	ACCOUNT #:
STARTING BALANCE:	PAYOFF DATE:
CREDIT LIMIT:	CREDIT TYPE:
INTEREST RATE: DUE DATE:	MIN PAYMENT:

Date	Starting Balance	Payment	End Balance	Confirmation No

Notes	

Debt Payoff

CREDITOR:		ACCOUNT #:	
STARTING BALANCE:		PAYOFF DATE:	
CREDIT LIMIT:		CREDIT TYPE:	
INTEREST RATE:	DUE DATE:	MIN PAYMENT:	

Date	Starting Balance	Payment	End Balance	Confirmation No

Notes	

Debt Payoff

CREDITOR:		ACCOUNT #:	
STARTING BALANCE:		PAYOFF DATE:	
CREDIT LIMIT:		CREDIT TYPE:	
INTEREST RATE:	DUE DATE:	MIN PAYMENT:	

Date	Starting Balance	Payment	End Balance	Confirmation No

Notes	

Debt Payoff

CREDITOR:		ACCOUNT #:	
STARTING BALANCE:		PAYOFF DATE:	
CREDIT LIMIT:		CREDIT TYPE:	
INTEREST RATE:	DUE DATE:	MIN PAYMENT:	

Date	Starting Balance	Payment	End Balance	Confirmation No

Notes	

Debt Payoff

CREDITOR:		ACCOUNT #:	
STARTING BALANCE:		PAYOFF DATE:	
CREDIT LIMIT:		CREDIT TYPE:	
INTEREST RATE:	DUE DATE:	MIN PAYMENT:	

Date	Starting Balance	Payment	End Balance	Confirmation No

Notes	

Debt Payoff

CREDITOR:	ACCOUNT #:
STARTING BALANCE:	PAYOFF DATE:
CREDIT LIMIT:	CREDIT TYPE:
INTEREST RATE:	DUE DATE:	MIN PAYMENT:

Date	Starting Balance	Payment	End Balance	Confirmation No

Notes	

Debt Payoff

CREDITOR:		ACCOUNT #:	
STARTING BALANCE:		PAYOFF DATE:	
CREDIT LIMIT:		CREDIT TYPE:	
INTEREST RATE:	DUE DATE:	MIN PAYMENT:	

Date	Starting Balance	Payment	End Balance	Confirmation No

Notes	

Debt Payoff

CREDITOR:		ACCOUNT #:	
STARTING BALANCE:		PAYOFF DATE:	
CREDIT LIMIT:		CREDIT TYPE:	
INTEREST RATE:	DUE DATE:	MIN PAYMENT:	

Date	Starting Balance	Payment	End Balance	Confirmation No

Notes	

Debt Payoff

CREDITOR:		ACCOUNT #:	
STARTING BALANCE:		PAYOFF DATE:	
CREDIT LIMIT:		CREDIT TYPE:	
INTEREST RATE:	DUE DATE:	MIN PAYMENT:	

Date	Starting Balance	Payment	End Balance	Confirmation No

Notes	

Debt Payoff

CREDITOR:		ACCOUNT #:	
STARTING BALANCE:		PAYOFF DATE:	
CREDIT LIMIT:		CREDIT TYPE:	
INTEREST RATE:	DUE DATE:	MIN PAYMENT:	

Date	Starting Balance	Payment	End Balance	Confirmation No

Notes	

Debt Payoff

CREDITOR:		ACCOUNT #:	
STARTING BALANCE:		PAYOFF DATE:	
CREDIT LIMIT:		CREDIT TYPE:	
INTEREST RATE:	DUE DATE:	MIN PAYMENT:	

Date	Starting Balance	Payment	End Balance	Confirmation No

Notes	

Debt Payoff

CREDITOR:		ACCOUNT #:	
STARTING BALANCE:		PAYOFF DATE:	
CREDIT LIMIT:		CREDIT TYPE:	
INTEREST RATE:	DUE DATE:	MIN PAYMENT:	

Date	Starting Balance	Payment	End Balance	Confirmation No

Notes	

Debt Payoff

CREDITOR:		ACCOUNT #:	
STARTING BALANCE:		PAYOFF DATE:	
CREDIT LIMIT:		CREDIT TYPE:	
INTEREST RATE:	DUE DATE:	MIN PAYMENT:	

Date	Starting Balance	Payment	End Balance	Confirmation No

Notes	

Debt Payoff

CREDITOR:		ACCOUNT #:	
STARTING BALANCE:		PAYOFF DATE:	
CREDIT LIMIT:		CREDIT TYPE:	
INTEREST RATE:	DUE DATE:	MIN PAYMENT:	

Date	Starting Balance	Payment	End Balance	Confirmation No

Notes	

Debt Payoff

CREDITOR:		ACCOUNT #:
STARTING BALANCE:		PAYOFF DATE:
CREDIT LIMIT:		CREDIT TYPE:
INTEREST RATE:	DUE DATE:	MIN PAYMENT:

Date	Starting Balance	Payment	End Balance	Confirmation No

Notes	

Debt Payoff

CREDITOR:		ACCOUNT #:	
STARTING BALANCE:		PAYOFF DATE:	
CREDIT LIMIT:		CREDIT TYPE:	
INTEREST RATE:	DUE DATE:	MIN PAYMENT:	

Date	Starting Balance	Payment	End Balance	Confirmation No

Notes	

Debt Payoff

CREDITOR:		ACCOUNT #:	
STARTING BALANCE:		PAYOFF DATE:	
CREDIT LIMIT:		CREDIT TYPE:	
INTEREST RATE:	DUE DATE:	MIN PAYMENT:	

Date	Starting Balance	Payment	End Balance	Confirmation No

Notes	

Debt Payoff

CREDITOR:		ACCOUNT #:	
STARTING BALANCE:		PAYOFF DATE:	
CREDIT LIMIT:		CREDIT TYPE:	
INTEREST RATE:	DUE DATE:	MIN PAYMENT:	

Date	Starting Balance	Payment	End Balance	Confirmation No

Notes	

Debt Payoff

CREDITOR:		ACCOUNT #:	
STARTING BALANCE:		PAYOFF DATE:	
CREDIT LIMIT:		CREDIT TYPE:	
INTEREST RATE:	DUE DATE:	MIN PAYMENT:	

Date	Starting Balance	Payment	End Balance	Confirmation No

Notes	

Debt Payoff

CREDITOR:		ACCOUNT #:	
STARTING BALANCE:		PAYOFF DATE:	
CREDIT LIMIT:		CREDIT TYPE:	
INTEREST RATE:	DUE DATE:	MIN PAYMENT:	

Date	Starting Balance	Payment	End Balance	Confirmation No

Notes	

Debt Payoff

CREDITOR:		ACCOUNT #:	
STARTING BALANCE:		PAYOFF DATE:	
CREDIT LIMIT:		CREDIT TYPE:	
INTEREST RATE:	DUE DATE:	MIN PAYMENT:	

Date	Starting Balance	Payment	End Balance	Confirmation No

Notes	

Debt Payoff

CREDITOR:		ACCOUNT #:	
STARTING BALANCE:		PAYOFF DATE:	
CREDIT LIMIT:		CREDIT TYPE:	
INTEREST RATE:	DUE DATE:	MIN PAYMENT:	

Date	Starting Balance	Payment	End Balance	Confirmation No

Notes	

Debt Payoff

CREDITOR:	ACCOUNT #:	
STARTING BALANCE:	PAYOFF DATE:	
CREDIT LIMIT:	CREDIT TYPE:	
INTEREST RATE:	DUE DATE:	MIN PAYMENT:

Date	Starting Balance	Payment	End Balance	Confirmation No

Notes	

Debt Payoff

CREDITOR:		ACCOUNT #:	
STARTING BALANCE:		PAYOFF DATE:	
CREDIT LIMIT:		CREDIT TYPE:	
INTEREST RATE:	DUE DATE:	MIN PAYMENT:	

Date	Starting Balance	Payment	End Balance	Confirmation No

Notes	

Debt Payoff

CREDITOR:		ACCOUNT #:	
STARTING BALANCE:		PAYOFF DATE:	
CREDIT LIMIT:		CREDIT TYPE:	
INTEREST RATE:	DUE DATE:		MIN PAYMENT:

Date	Starting Balance	Payment	End Balance	Confirmation No

Notes	

Debt Payoff

CREDITOR:		ACCOUNT #:	
STARTING BALANCE:		PAYOFF DATE:	
CREDIT LIMIT:		CREDIT TYPE:	
INTEREST RATE:	DUE DATE:	MIN PAYMENT:	

Date	Starting Balance	Payment	End Balance	Confirmation No

Notes	

Debt Payoff

CREDITOR:		ACCOUNT #:	
STARTING BALANCE:		PAYOFF DATE:	
CREDIT LIMIT:		CREDIT TYPE:	
INTEREST RATE:	DUE DATE:		MIN PAYMENT:

Date	Starting Balance	Payment	End Balance	Confirmation No

Notes	

Debt Payoff

CREDITOR:		ACCOUNT #:	
STARTING BALANCE:		PAYOFF DATE:	
CREDIT LIMIT:		CREDIT TYPE:	
INTEREST RATE:	DUE DATE:	MIN PAYMENT:	

Date	Starting Balance	Payment	End Balance	Confirmation No

Notes	

Debt Payoff

CREDITOR:		ACCOUNT #:	
STARTING BALANCE:		PAYOFF DATE:	
CREDIT LIMIT:		CREDIT TYPE:	
INTEREST RATE:	DUE DATE:	MIN PAYMENT:	

Date	Starting Balance	Payment	End Balance	Confirmation No

Notes	

Debt Payoff

CREDITOR:		ACCOUNT #:	
STARTING BALANCE:		PAYOFF DATE:	
CREDIT LIMIT:		CREDIT TYPE:	
INTEREST RATE:	DUE DATE:	MIN PAYMENT:	

Date	Starting Balance	Payment	End Balance	Confirmation No

Notes	

Debt Payoff

CREDITOR:		ACCOUNT #:	
STARTING BALANCE:		PAYOFF DATE:	
CREDIT LIMIT:		CREDIT TYPE:	
INTEREST RATE:	DUE DATE:	MIN PAYMENT:	

Date	Starting Balance	Payment	End Balance	Confirmation No

Notes	

Debt Payoff

CREDITOR:		ACCOUNT #:	
STARTING BALANCE:		PAYOFF DATE:	
CREDIT LIMIT:		CREDIT TYPE:	
INTEREST RATE:	DUE DATE:	MIN PAYMENT:	

Date	Starting Balance	Payment	End Balance	Confirmation No

Notes	

Debt Payoff

CREDITOR:		ACCOUNT #:	
STARTING BALANCE:		PAYOFF DATE:	
CREDIT LIMIT:		CREDIT TYPE:	
INTEREST RATE:	DUE DATE:	MIN PAYMENT:	

Date	Starting Balance	Payment	End Balance	Confirmation No

Notes	

Debt Payoff

CREDITOR:		ACCOUNT #:	
STARTING BALANCE:		PAYOFF DATE:	
CREDIT LIMIT:		CREDIT TYPE:	
INTEREST RATE:	DUE DATE:	MIN PAYMENT:	

Date	Starting Balance	Payment	End Balance	Confirmation No

Notes	

Debt Payoff

CREDITOR:		ACCOUNT #:		
STARTING BALANCE:		PAYOFF DATE:		
CREDIT LIMIT:		CREDIT TYPE:		
INTEREST RATE:	DUE DATE:		MIN PAYMENT:	

Date	Starting Balance	Payment	End Balance	Confirmation No

Notes	

Debt Payoff

CREDITOR:		ACCOUNT #:	
STARTING BALANCE:		PAYOFF DATE:	
CREDIT LIMIT:		CREDIT TYPE:	
INTEREST RATE:	DUE DATE:	MIN PAYMENT:	

Date	Starting Balance	Payment	End Balance	Confirmation No

Notes	

Debt Payoff

CREDITOR:		ACCOUNT #:	
STARTING BALANCE:		PAYOFF DATE:	
CREDIT LIMIT:		CREDIT TYPE:	
INTEREST RATE:	DUE DATE:	MIN PAYMENT:	

Date	Starting Balance	Payment	End Balance	Confirmation No

Notes	

Debt Payoff

CREDITOR:		ACCOUNT #:	
STARTING BALANCE:		PAYOFF DATE:	
CREDIT LIMIT:		CREDIT TYPE:	
INTEREST RATE:	DUE DATE:	MIN PAYMENT:	

Date	Starting Balance	Payment	End Balance	Confirmation No

Notes	

Debt Payoff

CREDITOR:		ACCOUNT #:	
STARTING BALANCE:		PAYOFF DATE:	
CREDIT LIMIT:		CREDIT TYPE:	
INTEREST RATE:	DUE DATE:		MIN PAYMENT:

Date	Starting Balance	Payment	End Balance	Confirmation No

Notes	

Debt Payoff

CREDITOR:		ACCOUNT #:	
STARTING BALANCE:		PAYOFF DATE:	
CREDIT LIMIT:		CREDIT TYPE:	
INTEREST RATE:	DUE DATE:	MIN PAYMENT:	

Date	Starting Balance	Payment	End Balance	Confirmation No

Notes	

Debt Payoff

CREDITOR:		ACCOUNT #:	
STARTING BALANCE:		PAYOFF DATE:	
CREDIT LIMIT:		CREDIT TYPE:	
INTEREST RATE:	DUE DATE:	MIN PAYMENT:	

Date	Starting Balance	Payment	End Balance	Confirmation No

Notes	

Debt Payoff

CREDITOR:		ACCOUNT #:	
STARTING BALANCE:		PAYOFF DATE:	
CREDIT LIMIT:		CREDIT TYPE:	
INTEREST RATE:	DUE DATE:		MIN PAYMENT:

Date	Starting Balance	Payment	End Balance	Confirmation No

Notes	

Debt Payoff

CREDITOR:		ACCOUNT #:	
STARTING BALANCE:		PAYOFF DATE:	
CREDIT LIMIT:		CREDIT TYPE:	
INTEREST RATE:	DUE DATE:	MIN PAYMENT:	

Date	Starting Balance	Payment	End Balance	Confirmation No

Notes	

Debt Payoff

CREDITOR:		ACCOUNT #:	
STARTING BALANCE:		PAYOFF DATE:	
CREDIT LIMIT:		CREDIT TYPE:	
INTEREST RATE:	DUE DATE:	MIN PAYMENT:	

Date	Starting Balance	Payment	End Balance	Confirmation No

Notes	

Debt Payoff

CREDITOR:		ACCOUNT #:	
STARTING BALANCE:		PAYOFF DATE:	
CREDIT LIMIT:		CREDIT TYPE:	
INTEREST RATE:	DUE DATE:	MIN PAYMENT:	

Date	Starting Balance	Payment	End Balance	Confirmation No

Notes	

Debt Payoff

CREDITOR:		ACCOUNT #:	
STARTING BALANCE:		PAYOFF DATE:	
CREDIT LIMIT:		CREDIT TYPE:	
INTEREST RATE:	DUE DATE:	MIN PAYMENT:	

Date	Starting Balance	Payment	End Balance	Confirmation No

Notes	

Debt Payoff

CREDITOR:		ACCOUNT #:	
STARTING BALANCE:		PAYOFF DATE:	
CREDIT LIMIT:		CREDIT TYPE:	
INTEREST RATE:	DUE DATE:	MIN PAYMENT:	

Date	Starting Balance	Payment	End Balance	Confirmation No

Notes	

Debt Payoff

CREDITOR:		ACCOUNT #:	
STARTING BALANCE:		PAYOFF DATE:	
CREDIT LIMIT:		CREDIT TYPE:	
INTEREST RATE:	DUE DATE:	MIN PAYMENT:	

Date	Starting Balance	Payment	End Balance	Confirmation No

Notes	

Debt Payoff

CREDITOR:		ACCOUNT #:	
STARTING BALANCE:		PAYOFF DATE:	
CREDIT LIMIT:		CREDIT TYPE:	
INTEREST RATE:	DUE DATE:	MIN PAYMENT:	

Date	Starting Balance	Payment	End Balance	Confirmation No

Notes	

Debt Payoff

CREDITOR:		ACCOUNT #:	
STARTING BALANCE:		PAYOFF DATE:	
CREDIT LIMIT:		CREDIT TYPE:	
INTEREST RATE:	DUE DATE:	MIN PAYMENT:	

Date	Starting Balance	Payment	End Balance	Confirmation No

Notes	

Debt Payoff

CREDITOR:		ACCOUNT #:	
STARTING BALANCE:		PAYOFF DATE:	
CREDIT LIMIT:		CREDIT TYPE:	
INTEREST RATE:	DUE DATE:	MIN PAYMENT:	

Date	Starting Balance	Payment	End Balance	Confirmation No

Notes	

Debt Payoff

CREDITOR:		ACCOUNT #:	
STARTING BALANCE:		PAYOFF DATE:	
CREDIT LIMIT:		CREDIT TYPE:	
INTEREST RATE:	DUE DATE:	MIN PAYMENT:	

Date	Starting Balance	Payment	End Balance	Confirmation No

Notes	

Debt Payoff

CREDITOR:		ACCOUNT #:	
STARTING BALANCE:		PAYOFF DATE:	
CREDIT LIMIT:		CREDIT TYPE:	
INTEREST RATE:	DUE DATE:	MIN PAYMENT:	

Date	Starting Balance	Payment	End Balance	Confirmation No

Notes	

Debt Payoff

CREDITOR:		ACCOUNT #:	
STARTING BALANCE:		PAYOFF DATE:	
CREDIT LIMIT:		CREDIT TYPE:	
INTEREST RATE:	DUE DATE:	MIN PAYMENT:	

Date	Starting Balance	Payment	End Balance	Confirmation No

Notes	

Debt Payoff

CREDITOR:		ACCOUNT #:	
STARTING BALANCE:		PAYOFF DATE:	
CREDIT LIMIT:		CREDIT TYPE:	
INTEREST RATE:	DUE DATE:	MIN PAYMENT:	

Date	Starting Balance	Payment	End Balance	Confirmation No

Notes	

Debt Payoff

CREDITOR:		ACCOUNT #:	
STARTING BALANCE:		PAYOFF DATE:	
CREDIT LIMIT:		CREDIT TYPE:	
INTEREST RATE:	DUE DATE:	MIN PAYMENT:	

Date	Starting Balance	Payment	End Balance	Confirmation No

Notes	

Debt Payoff

CREDITOR:		ACCOUNT #:	
STARTING BALANCE:		PAYOFF DATE:	
CREDIT LIMIT:		CREDIT TYPE:	
INTEREST RATE:	DUE DATE:	MIN PAYMENT:	

Date	Starting Balance	Payment	End Balance	Confirmation No

Notes	

Debt Payoff

CREDITOR:		ACCOUNT #:	
STARTING BALANCE:		PAYOFF DATE:	
CREDIT LIMIT:		CREDIT TYPE:	
INTEREST RATE:	DUE DATE:	MIN PAYMENT:	

Date	Starting Balance	Payment	End Balance	Confirmation No

Notes	

Debt Payoff

CREDITOR:		ACCOUNT #:
STARTING BALANCE:		PAYOFF DATE:
CREDIT LIMIT:		CREDIT TYPE:
INTEREST RATE:	DUE DATE:	MIN PAYMENT:

Date	Starting Balance	Payment	End Balance	Confirmation No

Notes

Debt Payoff

CREDITOR:		ACCOUNT #:	
STARTING BALANCE:		PAYOFF DATE:	
CREDIT LIMIT:		CREDIT TYPE:	
INTEREST RATE:	DUE DATE:	MIN PAYMENT:	

Date	Starting Balance	Payment	End Balance	Confirmation No

Notes

Debt Payoff

CREDITOR:		ACCOUNT #:	
STARTING BALANCE:		PAYOFF DATE:	
CREDIT LIMIT:		CREDIT TYPE:	
INTEREST RATE:	DUE DATE:	MIN PAYMENT:	

Date	Starting Balance	Payment	End Balance	Confirmation No

Notes	

Debt Payoff

CREDITOR:		ACCOUNT #:	
STARTING BALANCE:		PAYOFF DATE:	
CREDIT LIMIT:		CREDIT TYPE:	
INTEREST RATE:	DUE DATE:	MIN PAYMENT:	

Date	Starting Balance	Payment	End Balance	Confirmation No

Notes	

Debt Payoff

CREDITOR:		ACCOUNT #:	
STARTING BALANCE:		PAYOFF DATE:	
CREDIT LIMIT:		CREDIT TYPE:	
INTEREST RATE:	DUE DATE:	MIN PAYMENT:	

Date	Starting Balance	Payment	End Balance	Confirmation No

Notes	

Debt Payoff

CREDITOR:		ACCOUNT #:	
STARTING BALANCE:		PAYOFF DATE:	
CREDIT LIMIT:		CREDIT TYPE:	
INTEREST RATE:	DUE DATE:	MIN PAYMENT:	

Date	Starting Balance	Payment	End Balance	Confirmation No

Notes	

Debt Payoff

CREDITOR:		ACCOUNT #:	
STARTING BALANCE:		PAYOFF DATE:	
CREDIT LIMIT:		CREDIT TYPE:	
INTEREST RATE:	DUE DATE:	MIN PAYMENT:	

Date	Starting Balance	Payment	End Balance	Confirmation No

Notes	

Debt Payoff

CREDITOR:		ACCOUNT #:	
STARTING BALANCE:		PAYOFF DATE:	
CREDIT LIMIT:		CREDIT TYPE:	
INTEREST RATE:	DUE DATE:	MIN PAYMENT:	

Date	Starting Balance	Payment	End Balance	Confirmation No

Notes	

Debt Payoff

CREDITOR:		ACCOUNT #:	
STARTING BALANCE:		PAYOFF DATE:	
CREDIT LIMIT:		CREDIT TYPE:	
INTEREST RATE:	DUE DATE:		MIN PAYMENT:

Date	Starting Balance	Payment	End Balance	Confirmation No

Notes	

Debt Payoff

CREDITOR:		ACCOUNT #:	
STARTING BALANCE:		PAYOFF DATE:	
CREDIT LIMIT:		CREDIT TYPE:	
INTEREST RATE:	DUE DATE:	MIN PAYMENT:	

Date	Starting Balance	Payment	End Balance	Confirmation No

Notes	

Debt Payoff

CREDITOR:		ACCOUNT #:	
STARTING BALANCE:		PAYOFF DATE:	
CREDIT LIMIT:		CREDIT TYPE:	
INTEREST RATE:	DUE DATE:	MIN PAYMENT:	

Date	Starting Balance	Payment	End Balance	Confirmation No

Notes	

Debt Payoff

CREDITOR:		ACCOUNT #:	
STARTING BALANCE:		PAYOFF DATE:	
CREDIT LIMIT:		CREDIT TYPE:	
INTEREST RATE:	DUE DATE:	MIN PAYMENT:	

Date	Starting Balance	Payment	End Balance	Confirmation No

Notes	

Debt Payoff

CREDITOR:		ACCOUNT #:	
STARTING BALANCE:		PAYOFF DATE:	
CREDIT LIMIT:		CREDIT TYPE:	
INTEREST RATE:	DUE DATE:	MIN PAYMENT:	

Date	Starting Balance	Payment	End Balance	Confirmation No

Notes	

Debt Payoff

CREDITOR:		ACCOUNT #:	
STARTING BALANCE:		PAYOFF DATE:	
CREDIT LIMIT:		CREDIT TYPE:	
INTEREST RATE:	DUE DATE:	MIN PAYMENT:	

Date	Starting Balance	Payment	End Balance	Confirmation No

Notes	

Debt Payoff

CREDITOR:		ACCOUNT #:	
STARTING BALANCE:		PAYOFF DATE:	
CREDIT LIMIT:		CREDIT TYPE:	
INTEREST RATE:	DUE DATE:		MIN PAYMENT:

Date	Starting Balance	Payment	End Balance	Confirmation No

Notes	

Debt Payoff

CREDITOR:		ACCOUNT #:	
STARTING BALANCE:		PAYOFF DATE:	
CREDIT LIMIT:		CREDIT TYPE:	
INTEREST RATE:	DUE DATE:	MIN PAYMENT:	

Date	Starting Balance	Payment	End Balance	Confirmation No

Notes	

Debt Payoff

CREDITOR:		ACCOUNT #:	
STARTING BALANCE:		PAYOFF DATE:	
CREDIT LIMIT:		CREDIT TYPE:	
INTEREST RATE:	DUE DATE:	MIN PAYMENT:	

Date	Starting Balance	Payment	End Balance	Confirmation No

Notes	

Debt Payoff

CREDITOR:		ACCOUNT #:	
STARTING BALANCE:		PAYOFF DATE:	
CREDIT LIMIT:		CREDIT TYPE:	
INTEREST RATE:	DUE DATE:	MIN PAYMENT:	

Date	Starting Balance	Payment	End Balance	Confirmation No

Notes	

Debt Payoff

CREDITOR:		ACCOUNT #:	
STARTING BALANCE:		PAYOFF DATE:	
CREDIT LIMIT:		CREDIT TYPE:	
INTEREST RATE:	DUE DATE:	MIN PAYMENT:	

Date	Starting Balance	Payment	End Balance	Confirmation No

Notes	

Debt Payoff

CREDITOR:		ACCOUNT #:	
STARTING BALANCE:		PAYOFF DATE:	
CREDIT LIMIT:		CREDIT TYPE:	
INTEREST RATE:	DUE DATE:	MIN PAYMENT:	

Date	Starting Balance	Payment	End Balance	Confirmation No

Notes	

Debt Payoff

CREDITOR:		ACCOUNT #:	
STARTING BALANCE:		PAYOFF DATE:	
CREDIT LIMIT:		CREDIT TYPE:	
INTEREST RATE:	DUE DATE:	MIN PAYMENT:	

Date	Starting Balance	Payment	End Balance	Confirmation No

Notes	

Debt Payoff

CREDITOR:		ACCOUNT #:	
STARTING BALANCE:		PAYOFF DATE:	
CREDIT LIMIT:		CREDIT TYPE:	
INTEREST RATE:	DUE DATE:	MIN PAYMENT:	

Date	Starting Balance	Payment	End Balance	Confirmation No

Notes	

Debt Payoff

CREDITOR:		ACCOUNT #:	
STARTING BALANCE:		PAYOFF DATE:	
CREDIT LIMIT:		CREDIT TYPE:	
INTEREST RATE:	DUE DATE:		MIN PAYMENT:

Date	Starting Balance	Payment	End Balance	Confirmation No

Notes	

Debt Payoff

CREDITOR:		ACCOUNT #:	
STARTING BALANCE:		PAYOFF DATE:	
CREDIT LIMIT:		CREDIT TYPE:	
INTEREST RATE:	DUE DATE:	MIN PAYMENT:	

Date	Starting Balance	Payment	End Balance	Confirmation No

Notes	

Debt Payoff

CREDITOR:		ACCOUNT #:
STARTING BALANCE:		PAYOFF DATE:
CREDIT LIMIT:		CREDIT TYPE:
INTEREST RATE:	DUE DATE:	MIN PAYMENT:

Date	Starting Balance	Payment	End Balance	Confirmation No

Notes	

Debt Payoff

CREDITOR:		ACCOUNT #:	
STARTING BALANCE:		PAYOFF DATE:	
CREDIT LIMIT:		CREDIT TYPE:	
INTEREST RATE:	DUE DATE:	MIN PAYMENT:	

Date	Starting Balance	Payment	End Balance	Confirmation No

Notes	

Debt Payoff

CREDITOR:		ACCOUNT #:	
STARTING BALANCE:		PAYOFF DATE:	
CREDIT LIMIT:		CREDIT TYPE:	
INTEREST RATE:	DUE DATE:	MIN PAYMENT:	

Date	Starting Balance	Payment	End Balance	Confirmation No

Notes	

Debt Payoff

CREDITOR:		ACCOUNT #:	
STARTING BALANCE:		PAYOFF DATE:	
CREDIT LIMIT:		CREDIT TYPE:	
INTEREST RATE:	DUE DATE:	MIN PAYMENT:	

Date	Starting Balance	Payment	End Balance	Confirmation No

Notes	

Debt Payoff

CREDITOR:		ACCOUNT #:	
STARTING BALANCE:		PAYOFF DATE:	
CREDIT LIMIT:		CREDIT TYPE:	
INTEREST RATE:	DUE DATE:	MIN PAYMENT:	

Date	Starting Balance	Payment	End Balance	Confirmation No

Notes	

Debt Payoff

CREDITOR:		ACCOUNT #:	
STARTING BALANCE:		PAYOFF DATE:	
CREDIT LIMIT:		CREDIT TYPE:	
INTEREST RATE:	DUE DATE:	MIN PAYMENT:	

Date	Starting Balance	Payment	End Balance	Confirmation No

Notes	

Debt Payoff

CREDITOR:		ACCOUNT #:	
STARTING BALANCE:		PAYOFF DATE:	
CREDIT LIMIT:		CREDIT TYPE:	
INTEREST RATE:	DUE DATE:	MIN PAYMENT:	

Date	Starting Balance	Payment	End Balance	Confirmation No

Notes	

Debt Payoff

CREDITOR:		ACCOUNT #:	
STARTING BALANCE:		PAYOFF DATE:	
CREDIT LIMIT:		CREDIT TYPE:	
INTEREST RATE:	DUE DATE:	MIN PAYMENT:	

Date	Starting Balance	Payment	End Balance	Confirmation No

Notes	

Debt Payoff

CREDITOR:	ACCOUNT #:	
STARTING BALANCE:	PAYOFF DATE:	
CREDIT LIMIT:	CREDIT TYPE:	
INTEREST RATE:	DUE DATE:	MIN PAYMENT:

Date	Starting Balance	Payment	End Balance	Confirmation No

Notes	

Debt Payoff

CREDITOR:		ACCOUNT #:	
STARTING BALANCE:		PAYOFF DATE:	
CREDIT LIMIT:		CREDIT TYPE:	
INTEREST RATE:	DUE DATE:	MIN PAYMENT:	

Date	Starting Balance	Payment	End Balance	Confirmation No

Notes	

Debt Payoff

CREDITOR:		ACCOUNT #:	
STARTING BALANCE:		PAYOFF DATE:	
CREDIT LIMIT:		CREDIT TYPE:	
INTEREST RATE:	DUE DATE:		MIN PAYMENT:

Date	Starting Balance	Payment	End Balance	Confirmation No

Notes	

Debt Payoff

CREDITOR:		ACCOUNT #:	
STARTING BALANCE:		PAYOFF DATE:	
CREDIT LIMIT:		CREDIT TYPE:	
INTEREST RATE:	DUE DATE:	MIN PAYMENT:	

Date	Starting Balance	Payment	End Balance	Confirmation No

Notes	

Debt Payoff

CREDITOR:		ACCOUNT #:	
STARTING BALANCE:		PAYOFF DATE:	
CREDIT LIMIT:		CREDIT TYPE:	
INTEREST RATE:	DUE DATE:	MIN PAYMENT:	

Date	Starting Balance	Payment	End Balance	Confirmation No

Notes	

Debt Payoff

CREDITOR:	ACCOUNT #:
STARTING BALANCE:	PAYOFF DATE:
CREDIT LIMIT:	CREDIT TYPE:
INTEREST RATE:	DUE DATE:	MIN PAYMENT:

Date	Starting Balance	Payment	End Balance	Confirmation No

Notes	

Debt Payoff

CREDITOR:		ACCOUNT #:	
STARTING BALANCE:		PAYOFF DATE:	
CREDIT LIMIT:		CREDIT TYPE:	
INTEREST RATE:	DUE DATE:	MIN PAYMENT:	

Date	Starting Balance	Payment	End Balance	Confirmation No

Notes	

Debt Payoff

CREDITOR:		ACCOUNT #:	
STARTING BALANCE:		PAYOFF DATE:	
CREDIT LIMIT:		CREDIT TYPE:	
INTEREST RATE:	DUE DATE:	MIN PAYMENT:	

Date	Starting Balance	Payment	End Balance	Confirmation No

Notes	

Debt Payoff

CREDITOR:		ACCOUNT #:	
STARTING BALANCE:		PAYOFF DATE:	
CREDIT LIMIT:		CREDIT TYPE:	
INTEREST RATE:	DUE DATE:	MIN PAYMENT:	

Date	Starting Balance	Payment	End Balance	Confirmation No

Notes

Debt Payoff

CREDITOR:		ACCOUNT #:	
STARTING BALANCE:		PAYOFF DATE:	
CREDIT LIMIT:		CREDIT TYPE:	
INTEREST RATE:	DUE DATE:	MIN PAYMENT:	

Date	Starting Balance	Payment	End Balance	Confirmation No

Notes	

Debt Payoff

CREDITOR:		ACCOUNT #:	
STARTING BALANCE:		PAYOFF DATE:	
CREDIT LIMIT:		CREDIT TYPE:	
INTEREST RATE:	DUE DATE:	MIN PAYMENT:	

Date	Starting Balance	Payment	End Balance	Confirmation No

Notes	

Debt Payoff

CREDITOR:		ACCOUNT #:	
STARTING BALANCE:		PAYOFF DATE:	
CREDIT LIMIT:		CREDIT TYPE:	
INTEREST RATE:	DUE DATE:	MIN PAYMENT:	

Date	Starting Balance	Payment	End Balance	Confirmation No

Notes	

Debt Payoff

CREDITOR:		ACCOUNT #:	
STARTING BALANCE:		PAYOFF DATE:	
CREDIT LIMIT:		CREDIT TYPE:	
INTEREST RATE:	DUE DATE:	MIN PAYMENT:	

Date	Starting Balance	Payment	End Balance	Confirmation No

Notes	

Debt Payoff

CREDITOR:		ACCOUNT #:	
STARTING BALANCE:		PAYOFF DATE:	
CREDIT LIMIT:		CREDIT TYPE:	
INTEREST RATE:	DUE DATE:	MIN PAYMENT:	

Date	Starting Balance	Payment	End Balance	Confirmation No

Notes	

Debt Payoff

CREDITOR:		ACCOUNT #:	
STARTING BALANCE:		PAYOFF DATE:	
CREDIT LIMIT:		CREDIT TYPE:	
INTEREST RATE:	DUE DATE:	MIN PAYMENT:	

Date	Starting Balance	Payment	End Balance	Confirmation No

Notes	

Debt Payoff

CREDITOR:		ACCOUNT #:	
STARTING BALANCE:		PAYOFF DATE:	
CREDIT LIMIT:		CREDIT TYPE:	
INTEREST RATE:	DUE DATE:	MIN PAYMENT:	

Date	Starting Balance	Payment	End Balance	Confirmation No

Notes	

Debt Payoff

CREDITOR:	**ACCOUNT #:**	
STARTING BALANCE:	**PAYOFF DATE:**	
CREDIT LIMIT:	**CREDIT TYPE:**	
INTEREST RATE:	**DUE DATE:**	**MIN PAYMENT:**

Date	Starting Balance	Payment	End Balance	Confirmation No

Notes	

Made in the USA
Middletown, DE
02 September 2024

60224777R00064